Take Care

Take Care

by Mark Danowsky

~ 2025 ~

Take Care
© Copyright 2025 Mark Danowsky
All rights reserved. No part of this book may be used or reproduced in any manner whatsoever without written permission from either the author or the publisher, except in the case of credited epigraphs or brief quotations embedded in articles or reviews.

Editor-in-chief
Eric Morago

Operations Associate
Shelly Holder

Associate Editors
Mackensi E. Green
Ellen Webre
Allysa Murray

Editor Emeritus
Michael Miller

Front cover art
Aron Wiesenfeld

Book design
Michael Wada

Moon Tide logo design
Abraham Gomez

Take Care
is published by Moon Tide Press

Moon Tide Press
6709 Washington Ave. #9297
Whittier, CA 90608
www.moontidepress.com

FIRST EDITION

Printed in the United States of America

ISBN # 978-1-957799-32-2

for all the caregivers

Contents

Limerence	9
[a small shattering—]	10
Seams	11
Gathering	12
Eden	13
[how many trips now]	14
Magnetism	15
Lesson	16
Fear	17
You Have to Be Willing to Burn	18
Candle Reflections	19
[ghosts]	21
Lovelorn	22
Linger	23
Falling	24
Nudges	25
Sensuous	26
[your nude figure]	27
Liberation	28
Subconscious Deference	29
Grateful	30
Where You End & I Begin	31
Becoming Aware of the Tide	32
Matches	33
Not-Doing Everything	34
Average	35
Squash Blossoms	36
Rugged	37
Risk	38
The Spread	39
Bird in a Box	41
Grace	42
About the Author	43
Acknowledgements	44

Some days there might be nothing you encounter
To stand behind the fragile idea that anything matters
I feel as useless as a tree in a city park
Standing as a symbol of what we have blown apart

You know you break what you treasure
I tried to tell you
But I'm not sure you remember
So I tried to tell you

— The Weather Station

I'll follow you down,
but not that far

— Gin Blossoms

Tiny Resistance

I do not go
when asked to go

I spin the wheels
my thoughts, my silences

There is great loneliness
in ambiguous loss

Limerence

The joy
of a new on-
ramp———
short lived.

a small shattering—
fine layer of glass
over eggshells

Seams

That I can't see in a mirror
What can be pointed out

The frayed shirt collar
The holes around seams

My comfort taken over
Concern for others

Gathering

Back at my place
the next beer in hand
it's hard to say
if I went with intention
to build bridges
or burn

Eden

Finding the first garden
I painted its entrance
with Citronella

Keep Out
it now said
to nearly everything

how many trips now
I go & leave behind
a person with feelings
I am unsure I can reciprocate

Magnetism

Drawn
To others
In pain

Moth
Icarus-like
To flame

Lesson

You taught me
when you neglect them
plants thrive

How different we are

Fear

The one thing
I cannot protect you from
is yourself

You Have to Be Willing to Burn

What does it mean to scream
if you cannot breathe?

Candle Reflections

Sometimes it appears
the candle burns
at both ends

Sometimes it is a deception
the flame in the mirror
a reflection of yourself

Sometimes the candle
appears to burn
faster in reflection

Sometimes a lit candle
is just a candle in memory
of a life well-lived

Sometimes a candle burns
far too close to another
fast burning one of its own

Sometimes the light
of a twice lit candle
burns just right

Sometimes candle light
shines brighter in darkness
because it is so dark

Sometimes you don't know
all too well
until you see it burning bright

Sometimes once lit
a double image
glares in the mirror

Sometimes a candle
flames out
the only way it knows

ghosts
every town
I cannot rename

Lovelorn

must be nice

when we pine after each other

for good reasons

Linger

that scent
on your hands after
arranging tomatoes

Falling

She tells you
"You feel like Home"
& you have no choice
except fall in love

Nudges

If only
I could
know all
the ways
to make
your day
just that
much better

Sensuous

I see pain
Want to offer pleasure
Purple
Magnolia blossoms
Scattered
Petal angels

your nude figure
draped across me
shadowed contours on display
I read in near dark
just convinced
this is one form of unity

Liberation

Skin to skin, we write
a poem that has nothing to do
with the act, itself
a kind of poem, though not one
I'm eager to categorize
as free or formed—instead
let's try and focus on the facts:
goodness in the moment, light
scintillating without concern for direction

Subconscious Deference

You fake laugh at
something in your dream world
& I wonder who
deserves that level
of confirmation

Grateful

Easy to misunderstand
intentions to be a good host

The desire for confirmation
of success, told "well done"

Compliments, even half-hearted
ring true enough if need be

Where You End & I Begin

*On this occasion it's not true
look at me, I'm not you.*

— New Order

Under the mask of decision fatigue
and because I have a hand-me-down
gift card, I treat myself to gourmet coffee
at the end of the shopping trip
but almost pass on a blueberry scone
until I remember it's you
who does not like them

Becoming Aware of the Tide

Just today I feel older

Driving to the vet

Driving 17 miles for a hat I left behind
at a monthly meeting

Listening to a folk-rock album
awash in distracted serenity

Ebbing as soon
as it draws attention

Matches

next time you light one
watch how it reflects
opportunity

Not-Doing Everything

> *Practice not-doing / and everything*
> *will fall into place*
>
> — Tao Te Ching (Stephen Mitchell, trans.)

Straightaway this feels sinful.
But then, I wonder if monks suffer
from depression. Some must.
Nobody is just born.
I cannot come up with any nuances
in denial.

Average

Tao considers me average
from what I gather—
because I doubt.
This is fine by me
knowing what I know
about genius, I'm afraid
of what it would feel like to be one.
I rub my index finger over the edge
of my thumbnail—a habit I picked up
from watching a lowland gorilla at the zoo
who died on the operating table last year.
I miss that gorilla every time
I make this gesture. An average gesture
I am thankful for.

Squash Blossoms

How much do we owe
those in our orbit?

Better to give
delicacy over abundance?

Yellow and orange treats
versus big green

Wish I knew best
to give unto each

If only I was put here
as means to please

To please is all
consuming sometimes

But you keep me going
back to this garden

Rugged

little blemishes
on soft hands

minor injuries really
do build character

a reminder
I have a body

a reminder
I perform functions

Risk

The snow
melted
away today
as I typed
on forgetting
what it means
to be alive

The Spread

Through breaks in clouds

Tiny dots

Us going about our lives

Post-disaster

Tiny dots

Farther away

the living and the dead
do not compete
for the same real estate

Bird in a Box

Before I worked there
I saw a bird in the Walmart rafters
While browsing seed
For my feeders

I went to the hardware aisle
Retrieved a 28-cent box-cutter
And slit a cross

Subtle
I motioned to the bird

See how I try

Grace

Crows remember our faces
though we can't tell them apart

Some crows know water better than a child
but don't care how much of it we have

Elephants hear me as you see me—generic
rank among the broken
who rampage, who trample

All elephants learn touch soothes—
one places its trunk in another's mouth
taking in the silence

About the Author

Mark Danowsky is Editor-in-Chief of *ONE ART: a journal of poetry* and Poetry Craft Essays Editor for *Cleaver Magazine*. His poetry collections include *Meatless* (Plan B Press), *Violet Flame* (tiny wren lit), *JAWN* (Moonstone Press), and *As Falls Trees* (Night Ballet Press).

Acknowledgements

Tiny Resistance appeared in Violet Flame (tiny wren lit, 2022)
Seams appeared in Indian Voice Journal in 2016
Gathering appeared in Violet Flame (tiny wren lit, 2022)
Eden appeared in Violet Flame (tiny wren lit, 2022)
[how many trips now] appeared in CAREEN
    (Origami Poems Project microchap)
Magnetism appeared in Violet Flame (tiny wren lit, 2022)
Lesson appeared in Violet Flame (tiny wren lit, 2022)
You Have To Be Willing to Burn appeared in Violet Flame
    (tiny wren lit, 2022)
Candlelight Reflections appeared in Violet Flame
    (tiny wren lit, 2022)
ghosts appeared in Violet Flame (tiny wren lit, 2022)
Lovelorn appeared in CAREEN
    (Origami Poems Project microchap)
Linger appeared in ENDLESS LOVE
    (Origami Poems Project microchap)
Nudges appeared in ENDLESS LOVE
    (Origami Poems Project microchap)
Sensuous appeared in ENDLESS LOVE
    (Origami Poems Project microchap)
[your nude figure] appeared in ENDLESS LOVE
    (Origami Poems Project microchap)
Liberation appeared in ENDLESS LOVE
    (Origami Poems Project microchap)
Subconscious Deference appeared in Violet Flame
    (tiny wren lit, 2022)
Grateful appeared in The Best of Kindness II, 2017,
    Origami Poems Press
Where You End & I Begin appeared in Poppy Road Review in 2015
Becoming Aware of The Tide appeared in Burningword Literary
    Journal in 2016
Matches appeared in Violet Flame (tiny wren lit, 2022)
Not-Doing Everything appeared in Message in a Bottle (UK)
Average appeared in "Civilized Beasts," an anthology by
    Weasel Press

Squash Blossoms appeared in Peacock Journal
Rugged appeared in Alba: A Journal of Short Poetry in 2013
Risk appeared in bottle rockets in 2012
The Spread appeared in Red Eft Review
the living and the dead appeared in Otoliths in 2020 and Violet Flame
    (tiny wren lit, 2022)
Bird in a Box appeared in Gargoyle
Grace appeared in Gargoyle

~ Special Thanks ~

Special thanks to Donna Hilbert, James Crews, Faith Shearin, Louisa Schnaithmann, and Eric Morago. A big thank you to the many poets, writers, editors, colleagues, friends, who have encouraged and supported my personal writing, as well as my literary community efforts, along the way.

Also Available from Moon Tide Press

Dilapitatia, Kelly Gray (2025)
Reluctant Prophets, J.D. Isip (2025)
Enormous Blue Umbrella, Donna Hilbert (2025)
Sky Leaning Toward Winter, Terri Niccum (2024)
Living the Sundown: A Caregiving Memoir, G. Murray Thomas (2024)
Figure Study, Kathryn de Lancellotti (2024)
Suffer for This: Love, Sex, Marriage, & Rock 'N' Roll, Victor D. Infante (2024)
What Blooms in the Dark, Emily J. Mundy (2024)
Fable, Bryn Wickerd (2024)
Diamond Bars 2, David A. Romero (2024)
Safe Handling, Rebecca Evans (2024)
More Jerkumstances: New & Selected Poems, Barbara Eknoian (2024)
Dissection Day, Ally McGregor (2023)
He's a Color Until He's Not, Christian Hanz Lozada (2023)
The Language of Fractions, Nicelle Davis (2023)
Paradise Anonymous, Oriana Ivy (2023)
Now You Are a Missing Person, Susan Hayden (2023)
Maze Mouth, Brian Sonia-Wallace (2023)
Tangled by Blood, Rebecca Evans (2023)
Another Way of Loving Death, Jeremy Ra (2023)
Kissing the Wound, J.D. Isip (2023)
Feed It to the River, Terhi K. Cherry (2022)
Beat Not Beat: An Anthology of California Poets Screwing on the Beat and Post-Beat Tradition (2022)
When There Are Nine: Poems Celebrating the Life and Achievements of Ruth Bader Ginsburg (2022)
The Knife Thrower's Daughter, Terri Niccum (2022)
2 Revere Place, Aruni Wijesinghe (2022)
Here Go the Knives, Kelsey Bryan-Zwick (2022)
Trumpets in the Sky, Jerry Garcia (2022)
Threnody, Donna Hilbert (2022)
A Burning Lake of Paper Suns, Ellen Webre (2021)
Instructions for an Animal Body, Kelly Gray (2021)
*Head *V* Heart: New & Selected Poems*, Rob Sturma (2021)
Sh!t Men Say to Me: A Poetry Anthology in Response to Toxic Masculinity (2021)
Flower Grand First, Gustavo Hernandez (2021)

Everything is Radiant Between the Hates, Rich Ferguson (2020)
When the Pain Starts: Poetry as Sequential Art, Alan Passman (2020)
This Place Could Be Haunted If I Didn't Believe in Love,
    Lincoln McElwee (2020)
Impossible Thirst, Kathryn de Lancellotti (2020)
Lullabies for End Times, Jennifer Bradpiece (2020)
Crabgrass World, Robin Axworthy (2020)
Contortionist Tongue, Dania Ayah Alkhouli (2020)
The only thing that makes sense is to grow, Scott Ferry (2020)
Dead Letter Box, Terri Niccum (2019)
Tea and Subtitles: Selected Poems 1999-2019, Michael Miller (2019)
At the Table of the Unknown, Alexandra Umlas (2019)
The Book of Rabbits, Vince Trimboli (2019)
Everything I Write Is a Love Song to the World, David McIntire (2019)
Letters to the Leader, HanaLena Fennel (2019)
Darwin's Garden, Lee Rossi (2019)
Dark Ink: A Poetry Anthology Inspired by Horror (2018)
Drop and Dazzle, Peggy Dobreer (2018)
Junkie Wife, Alexis Rhone Fancher (2018)
The Moon, My Lover, My Mother, & the Dog, Daniel McGinn (2018)
Lullaby of Teeth: An Anthology of Southern California Poetry (2017)
Angels in Seven, Michael Miller (2016)
A Likely Story, Robbi Nester (2014)
Embers on the Stairs, Ruth Bavetta (2014)
The Green of Sunset, John Brantingham (2013)
The Savagery of Bone, Timothy Matthew Perez (2013)
The Silence of Doorways, Sharon Venezio (2013)
Cosmos: An Anthology of Southern California Poetry (2012)
Straws and Shadows, Irena Praitis (2012)
In the Lake of Your Bones, Peggy Dobreer (2012)
I Was Building Up to Something, Susan Davis (2011)
Hopeless Cases, Michael Kramer (2011)
One World, Gail Newman (2011)
What We Ache For, Eric Morago (2010)
Now and Then, Lee Mallory (2009)
Pop Art: An Anthology of Southern California Poetry (2009)
In the Heaven of Never Before, Carine Topal (2008)
A Wild Region, Kate Buckley (2008)
Carving in Bone: An Anthology of Orange County Poetry (2007)

Kindness from a Dark God, Ben Trigg (2007)
A Thin Strand of Lights, Ricki Mandeville (2006)
Sleepyhead Assassins, Mindy Nettifee (2006)
Tide Pools: An Anthology of Orange County Poetry (2006)
Lost American Nights: Lyrics & Poems, Michael Ubaldini (2006)

Patrons

Moon Tide Press would like to thank the following people for their support in helping publish the finest poetry from the Southern California region. To sign up as a patron, visit www.moontidepress.com or send an email to publisher@moontidepress.com.

Anonymous
Robin Axworthy
Conner Brenner
Nicole Connolly
Bill Cushing
Susan Davis
Kristen Baum DeBeasi
Peggy Dobreer
Kate Gale
Dennis Gowans
Alexis Rhone Fancher
HanaLena Fennel
Half Off Books & Brad T. Cox
Donna Hilbert
Jim & Vicky Hoggatt
Michael Kramer
Ron Koertge & Bianca Richards
Gary Jacobelly
Ray & Christi Lacoste

Jeffery Lewis
Zachary & Tammy Locklin
Lincoln McElwee
David McIntire
José Enrique Medina
Michael Miller &
Rachanee Srisavasdi
Michelle & Robert Miller
Ronny & Richard Morago
Terri Niccum
Andrew November
Jeremy Ra
Luke & Mia Salazar
Jennifer Smith
Roger Sponder
Andrew Turner
Rex Wilder
Mariano Zaro
Wes Bryan Zwick

www.ingramcontent.com/pod-product-compliance
Lightning Source LLC
Chambersburg PA
CBHW021001090426
42736CB00010B/1412